20TH CENTURY · DESIGN

70s AND 80s

THE HIGH-TECH AGE

Jackie Gaff and John Tyrrell

Heinemann
LIBRARY

CONTENTS

21712522

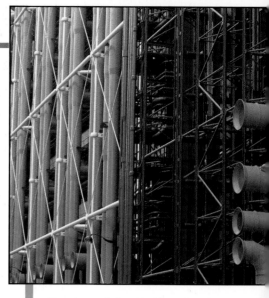

Designed by Italian Renzo Piano and Briton Richard Rogers, and opened in '77, Paris's high-tech Pompidou Centre turned architecture inside out and the design establishment upside down.

In '81, the American space agency NASA launched the first-ever reuseable spacecraft, the space shuttle Columbia, in a blaze of publicity.

20TH CENTURY · DESIGN

70s AND 80s

THE HIGH-TECH AGE

20TH CENTURY DESIGN – '70s and '80s
was produced by

David West ♟ **Children's Books**
7 Princeton Court
55 Felsham Road
London SW15 1AZ

Picture Research: Brooks Krikler Research

First published in Great Britain in 1999 by
Heinemann Library, Halley Court, Jordan Hill,
Oxford OX2 8EJ, a division of Reed Educational and
Professional Publishing Limited.

OXFORD MELBOURNE AUCKLAND
JOHANNESBURG BLANTYRE GABORONE
IBADAN PORTSMOUTH (NH) USA CHICAGO

Copyright © 1999 David West Children's Books

03 02 01 00 99
10 9 8 7 6 5 4 3 2 1

ISBN 0 431 03958 5 (HB)
ISBN 0 431 03959 3 (PB)

British Library Cataloguing in Publication Data

Gaff, Jackie
High-tech age (1970s-1980s). - (Design in the
twentieth century)
1. Design - History - 20th century - Juvenile literature
I. Title
745.4'442

Printed and bound in Italy

PHOTO CREDITS :
Abbreviations: t-top, m-middle, b-bottom,
r-right, l-left, c-centre.

Cover tl, mc & br, 4t, 5ml, 12-13, 13,
15b, 16, 17bm, 18m, 18-19, 19 20 -
Corbis. Cover tr & bl, 5mr, 21t, 25tr &
27t - Solution Pictures. Cover ml & 6br -
Patrick Demarchelier © Vogue/Condé
Nast publications Ltd. Cover bc, 6-7, 9t,
11t, 18b, 24 both, 25tl & m, 27bl & br -
Frank Spooner Pictures. 3, 4b, 28 all &
29 all - NASA. 5br E.Echenberg/Redferns.
6m & 8br - Arthur Elgort ©Vogue/Condé
Nast publications. 6bl - G. Chin/
Redferns. 7m - Lothar Schmid
©Vogue/Condé Nast publications. 7bl -
Willie Christie ©Vogue/Condé Nast
publications. 7br - J. Krsteske/Redferns.
9m - Alitalia. 8l - Eye Ubiquitous. 11b -
Dyson. 14m - courtesy of Wolfgang
Weingart. 14-15 - Paul Nightingale. 15t -
Redferns. 16-17 - Norman McGrath. 17tr
- Clare Oliver. 17br - Kobal Collection.
20-21t - GEC Computers Ltd. 20-21b -
Apple Macintosh. 22t - JVC. 22b -
Science & Society. 23t - Olivetti. 23m -
Braun. 26 both & 26-27 - Airbus.

*The dates in brackets after a designer's
name give the years that he or she lived.
Where a date appears after an object (or, in
the case of a building, the town where it is
situated), it is the year of its design.
'C.' stands for circa, meaning about or
approximately.*

*An explanation of difficult words can be
found in the glossary on page 30.*

TURBULENT TIMES

The 1970s and '80s were decades of rapid and often violent change. Wars in Vietnam, the Middle East, the Falklands and Afghanistan were part of a general climate of political unrest. This ranged from the struggle by women, gays and blacks for social equality to the PLO and IRA's terrorist campaigns, and from the Watergate scandal to the assassination of the Indian and Egyptian heads of government.

Economies swung between boom and bust, as nations battled with the oil crisis of the early '70s, sank into recession, and recovered to enjoy the high-rolling '80s. Then, on 19th October '87, another era of financial insecurity was ushered in by the Black Monday stock market collapse.

An electronic revolution was taking place, as microprocessors transformed everything from the space programme to the domestic washing machine. Design and architecture were also being turned inside out, as the severe formality of modernism was exploded by the wit of the post-modernists and the anarchy of the punks.

The 'I love New York' logo is one of the 1970s' most enduring symbols.

Micro-processors first went on sale in '71.

Computer-controlled robots revolutionized industry in the '70s and '80s.

Designed by Michael Graves, this kettle is one of the most famous products of post-modernism.

Punk style was deliberately shocking – an expression of the anger and frustration felt by many during the high employment of the '70s.

FASHION FREEDOM

In fashion, as in other design fields, the '70s and '80s were decades of extremes. Styles changed almost daily, as people pushed freedom of expression to the limits.

GOING TO EXTREMES

The anti-war protesters of the '70s mocked the military by adopting army surplus gear, while some gays and feminists confused ideas about masculinity by flaunting macho styles or workwear such as dungarees. Others responded to rising unemployment and social inequality by escaping into fantasy, glamour or nostalgia for the past. Some of the most outrageous trends were set by glam rockers such as Marc Bolan – hair got longer, platform boots got higher and flared trousers got ever wider.

Flares were revived at the end of the '80s, as retro designers reinterpreted '60s and '70s styles.

John Travolta boogied on down in Saturday Night Fever *('78), as discomania swept the world.*

BOYS WILL BE GIRLS WILL BE BOYS

Unisex was a constant theme throughout the '60s and '70s, but by the end of the '80s the fashion was for androgyny (looking both masculine and feminine) – as girls dressed as boys, and boys as girls.

Pop singer Boy George was the most famous gender-bender of the '80s.

An outfit by Rei Kawakubo from '88, the year she declared 'red is the new black'.

6

TECHNOLOGICAL DEVELOPMENTS IN TEXTILE PRODUCTION

Introduced by the Du Pont company in 1958, Lycra is the trademark of a synthetic elastic fibre. To maximize its stretch and strength, and improve its feel and the way it hangs, Lycra is always mixed with another fibre (shown right in purple). The different ways of doing this include covering it with the other fibre (1); twisting it with the other fibre as it is spun (2); or forcing it through an air jet with the other fibre, coating it in a lacework of strands (3).

DISCO BABES & PUNKS

Synthetic fabrics such as stretchy Lycra came into their own in the '70s, as the passion for working out took hold and discomania set in. At the other extreme was the anti-fashion brigade, the punks, with their ripped clothes and safety-pin jewellery.

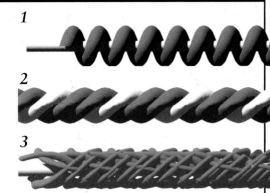

When punk met haute couture in Zandra Rhodes' Punk Chic collection of '77, the safety pins were gold!

WEST MEETS EAST

By the early '80s, the frilly shirts of the new romantics heralded a shift towards the nostalgia of retro styles – in sharp contrast to the masculine, padded-shouldered power suits worn by yuppie businesswomen of the period. Meanwhile Japanese designers such as Issey Miyake (*b.*'35), Rei Kawakubo (*b.*'42) and Yohji Yamamoto (*b.*'43) were revolutionizing the whole idea of tailored clothing, by draping and layering fabrics to create sculptural works of art.

With feathered hats and lace shirts, the new romantics of the early '80s turned into swashbuckling pirates.

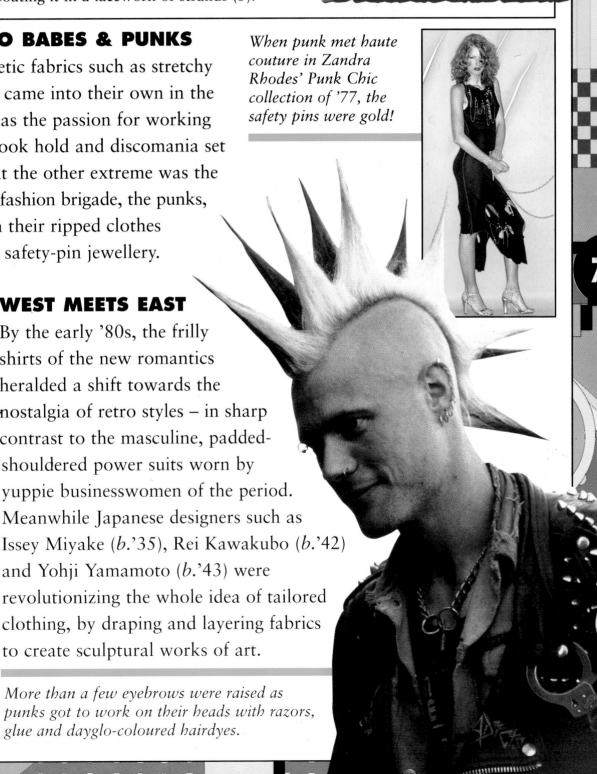

More than a few eyebrows were raised as punks got to work on their heads with razors, glue and dayglo-coloured hairdyes.

SPORTS TECHNOLOGY

Keeping fit became a worldwide obsession during the '70s and '80s, as thousands of people took up aerobics, weight-lifting, jogging, cycling, rollerskating or even marathon running. The mania was fed by new sports and the development of high-tech clothes and equipment.

The frames of high-tech mountain bikes are made from lightweight aluminium, titanium, or carbon-fibre-reinforced plastics.

CLIMB EVERY MOUNTAIN

Like many of the new sports of the period, mountain biking was born in California, in the United States. In the '60s, motorcyclists were banned from dirt tracks in the State's national parks. The bikers responded by shifting to bicycles, rapidly customizing their machines to cope with the rugged conditions. The distinctive design of these new machines included flat, motorbike-style handlebars, sturdy frames, strong brakes, fat tyres – and, of course, lots of low gears for getting to the top of all those mountains.

Skateboards were first manufactured in the United States in the '60s. The sport took off internationally during the '70s.

Inline skates were invented in the late '70s, when an ice-hockey player wanted skates he could train on in summer as well as in winter.

8

Microlights are hang-gliders that are powered by an engine. They were introduced in the early '70s, and developed out of the growing popularity of the sport of hang-gliding.

9

FLYING WITH THE BIRDS

The history of hang-gliding dates back to the 1890s, when the German engineer Otto Lilienthal (1848–96) built and tested a series of hang-glider-like machines in his pioneering efforts to unlock the secrets of heavier-than-air flight. The modern sport of hang-gliding took off in California, USA, in the 1960s, and was encouraged by the development of high-tech materials such as the strong and lightweight carbon-fibre-reinforced plastics.

Otto Lilienthal made over 2,000 glider flights before tragically plummeting to his death in 1896.

LIGHTWEIGHT TECHNOLOGY

Sport usually means speed, and reducing weight is a surefire way of delivering a winning edge. The big technological breakthroughs of the period lay in the introduction of strong, but lightweight materials such as carbon-fibre-reinforced plastics. Carbon-fibre-reinforced plastics are much lighter than steel, but can be up to eight times as strong. They were developed in the '60s and were soon being used in place of steel in a wide range of sporting equipment, from mountain bikes to hang-gliders and racing cars, as well as in the space and aircraft industries.

CARBON FIBRE – THE LIGHTWEIGHT HEAVYWEIGHT

Carbon-fibre-reinforced plastics are made by reinforcing plastic with carbon fibre. Carbon fibres were first made in the 1960s at the Farnborough Aircraft Establishment in Britain. They are very strong because of their crystalline structure – inside each hair-like fibre, the tiny carbon crystals are bonded together in long rows. Even stronger than individual fibres are carbon-fibre laminates, in which layers of the fibres are built up at angles to one another.

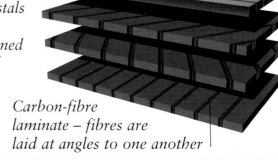

Carbon fibre – crystals are aligned

Carbon-fibre laminate – fibres are laid at angles to one another

POST-MODERNISM

The word post-modernism means 'after modernism', and it is used to describe the reaction to the modernist style that had dominated architecture and design for much of the 20th century.

LESS IS MORE

Modernists believed that form should follow function – that the appearance of an object or building should be determined by its use. They rejected historical styles and unnecessary decoration in favour of purely functional, geometric forms and neutral colours such as black and white. Modernist theory was summarized by the saying 'less is more', coined by one of the leading modernist architects, the German-born American Mies van der Rohe (1886–1969). His most famous building is the Seagram tower (New York, '59) – a stark rectangle of smoked-brown glass and bronze-finished steel beams.

Exotically named the Cairo table, this colourful piece of furniture was created by the post-modern Italian architect-designer Michele De Lucchi (b.'51) in '86.

LESS IS A BORE

In the mid-'60s the growing revolt against this tasteful minimalism was encapsulated by the phrase 'less is a bore', made in response to Mies van der Rohe's saying by another American architect, Robert Venturi (b.'25). Over the next two decades post-modernists such as Venturi argued that buildings and objects should be more than simply functional.

The little plastic bird on this whistling kettle's spout sings when the water boils. This humorous post-modern icon was created in '85 by the American architect and designer Michael Graves (b.'34), for the Italian manufacturers Alessi.

10

The soft, almost toy-like shapes and vibrant colours of this prototype electric fire are the epitome of post-modernism (Michele De Lucchi, early '80s).

Vacuum cleaners came in serious, sombre colours until James Dyson's bagless machines hit the market in '84.

They believed that modernism was cool and emotionless, preferring decoration and historical references in their designs. They felt that designs should stir memories and emotions; that by doing so they become more attractive to those using or looking at them.

ANYTHING GOES

Above all else, post-modernism was stimulating. Designs were witty, playful and ironic, colourful and eclectic (or wide-ranging). Themes were not only borrowed from past times, but also embraced contemporary fashions, while distinctions between good taste and kitsch, high art and popular culture were exploded. Shapes might be geometric or organic (based on living things), while decoration might be plain, bright colours or a riot of pattern and texture. And as form was freed from function, objects no longer needed to be useful – they could just be fashionable!

French designer Philippe Starck (b.'49) created this office stool for the German film director Wim Wenders (WW stool, '90). The playful contrast between organic form (it looks like the roots of a living plant) and non-organic materials (it is made from lacquered aluminium) is typically post-modern.

DYSON'S DUAL CYCLONE

It took British designer James Dyson (b.'47) five years and 5,127 prototypes to develop his revolutionary bagless vacuum cleaner. The first model, the G Force, was produced in Japan in '84 and sold for £1,200! The income from this allowed Dyson to open his own research centre and factory in Britain in the '90s, and to develop the Dual Cyclone (DC) models. Dyson's DC system replaced the traditional filter bag with two cyclone chambers. Inside the chambers, air spins at over 1,450 km/h, generating a mini-tornado that sucks up the dust particles.

FANTASY FURNISHINGS

Post-modern ideas freed designers to take a radically fresh look at furniture and interior design. Rules went out of the window, as rich decoration was combined with minimalist forms, and expensive materials with kitsch colour and pattern.

The circles and cones of this table lamp recall the geometric forms of modernist design classics, but the use of brilliantly coloured glass is very definitely post-modern (Ettore Sottsass, Bay table lamp, '83).

Made from wood and plastic laminates, Ettore Sottsass's lurid Carlton sideboard was inspired by '50s coffee-bar interiors and Aztec art. Sottsass created the piece for the Memphis group's first exhibition in '81.

DESIGN DYNAMITE

The Italian design group Memphis burst on to the international stage in September '81 with their first exhibition of post-modern furnishings. Memphis was the most influential new design movement of the decade, and the group had enormous impact worldwide. The group's founding father was the Italian architect and designer Ettore Sottsass (*b.*'17), and other founder members included Italian Michele De Lucchi, Briton George Sowden (*b.*'42) and Frenchwoman Nathalie du Pasquier (*b.*'57). Other post-modern designers, including Japan's Shiro Kuramata ('34–91) and Britain's Michael Graves, also created occasional pieces for the group.

ELVIS RULES OKAY

The group's name was typical of their eclectic approach. Before it became famous as the city in Tennessee, USA, where blues music was born and Elvis Presley built his home Graceland, Memphis had been one of the capital cities of ancient Egypt.

THE NEW DESIGN

Memphis designers took inspiration from historical and popular culture – Ancient Egypt, the Aztecs, comic strips, punk, children's toys – and combined it with bizarre materials to turn ideas of good taste upside down. Typical of Memphis's jumbling of 'high' and 'low' style was their use of colourful plastic laminates such as Formica – before this, laminates had been relegated to cafés and coffee bars.

With its elegant proportions and innovative form, this 'wavy' chest of drawers made Japanese designer Shiro Kuramata world famous (Furniture in Irregular Forms, '70). In the '80s, Kuramata created pieces for the Memphis group, including a concrete table embedded with coloured-glass pieces.

THE NEW SIMPLICITY

Memphis may have been the loudest new design style of the period, but it wasn't, of course, the only one. Designers such as Italian Gae Aulenti (*b.*'27), Israeli Ron Arad (*b.*'51) and Briton Tom Dixon (*b.*'59) created simpler, more sculptural pieces from industrial materials such as iron, steel, sheet glass and rubber.

STREET STYLE

British designer and businessman Terence Conran (*b.*'31) brought interior design to the high street when he opened his first Habitat shop in London's Fulham Road in '64. Habitat sold everything from furniture to curtain fabrics and cutlery, and the look was an instant success. In the '80s, Conran backed his belief in good design through the Conran Foundation, which funded the Design Museum that opened in London in '89.

The variety of colour and form of the furniture and lighting is typically post-modernist in this '80s apartment of Chicago furniture designer Cockrell.

Gae Aulenti is one of the few female architect-designers to achieve international fame. With this piece, she gave the traditional glass top of a coffee table a high-tech twist, by supporting it on industrial, metal-and-rubber castors (Table With Wheels, '80).

Terence Conran photographed in one of his apartments in '81.

GRAPHICS

Post-modernism and punk sent shock waves through the design establishment, as radical graphic designers experimented with the typography and page layout of books, magazines and posters.

Wolfgang Weingart layered type and images to create this poster for an exhibition of the modernist designer Herbert Bayer's work ('82).

LEADER OF THE PACK

Perhaps the most influential graphic designer of the period was German-born Wolfgang Weingart (*b.*'41), who began teaching typography at a leading Swiss design school in '68. Weingart challenged nearly every type convention of the day, opening up letter and word spacing, changing type weight in mid-word, and collaging type and images. His ideas were spread internationally by his students, one of whom was American graphic designer April Greiman (*b.*'48).

Advertizing campaigns such as Benetton's 'united colors' posters tried to exploit the shock value of social taboos.

I ♥ NY

A symbol replaced the word 'love' for the first time in this famous logo, created in '77 by the American Milton Glaser (b.'29).

Visual symbols could also be built into type, thanks to cheaper photo-typesetting (children's typeface by British designer Richard Ward, '77).

ABCDEFGHIJKLMNOPQRSTUVWXYZ

14

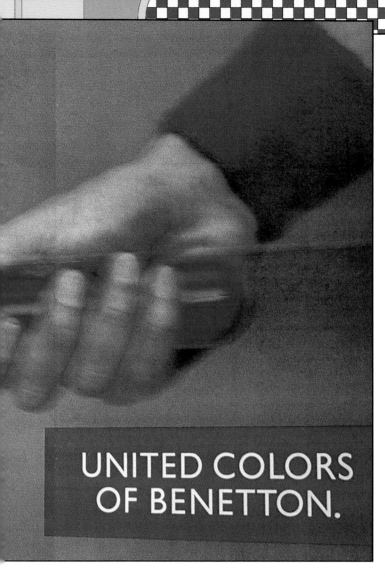

UNITED COLORS
OF BENETTON.

Jamie Reid began art directing for the Sex Pistols when they were founded in '75 (record sleeve, '77). His use of cut-out blackmail letters and vivid, clashing colours captured the chaos of punk.

NEVER MIND
THE BOLLOCKS
HERE'S THE
Sex Pistols

ANARCHY IN THE UK

In Britain, the anarchic force of punk music found expression in the ripped-and-pasted designs of Jamie Reid (*b.*'40). Another original British designer of the period was Neville Brody (*b.*'57), art director of *The Face* magazine in '81–86. Brody's unconventional page layouts and use of specially created logos and typefaces were mimicked worldwide.

MAKING 3-D PICTURES WITH LASERS

One of the new technologies available to advertizing agencies and graphic designers during this period was the hologram – a kind of 3-D photograph dreamt up in 1947, but not made possible until the first working laser was developed in '60. To make a hologram, mirrors are used to split laser light into a reference beam and one or more object beams. The reference beam is directed straight at a special photographic plate, while the object beams are bounced off the object towards the plate. Interference between the reference and object beams makes patterns on the plate which can later be viewed as a hologram.

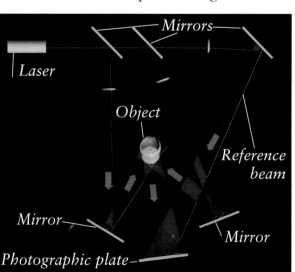

Mirrors
Laser
Object
Reference beam
Mirror
Mirror
Photographic plate

A hologram was used on the cover of National Geographic *magazine in '85.*

VOL. 168, NO. 5 — NOVEMBER 1985
DOUBLE MAP SUPPLEMENT: CANADA AND ITS VACATIONLANDS
NATIONAL GEOGRAPHIC
Holographic image of Africa's Taung child, one to two million years old
THE SEARCH FOR EARLY MAN
OFFICIAL JOURNAL OF THE NATIONAL GEOGRAPHIC SOCIETY WASHINGTON

ARCHITECTURE

The work of post-modern architects ranged from the elegant to the surreal, and if any one aim united them it was expressed by the American Philip Johnson (*b*.1906) when he said: 'have fun, always try to get fun in.' Johnson had worked with Mies van der Rohe on his severely modernist Seagram tower. However, by the early '80s Johnson's experiments with different architectural styles had led him in a new direction.

The shape of this skyscraper quickly earned it the nickname of the Lipstick building. Designed by Philip Johnson, it is made from red granite, glass and aluminium (New York, '86).

FATHER OF POST-MODERNISM

Another of Johnson's sayings was 'we were getting bored of the box', and his 197-metre-high, pink granite AT&T building (New York, '78–84) certainly broke the mould. It was the first major post-modern building, and various critics have compared it with a grandfather clock, a gravestone, and the front end of a Rolls Royce. Other leading American post-modern architects included Robert Venturi, Charles Moore (*b*.'25) and Michael Graves (who designed the Kettle with bird for Alessi).

A POST-MODERN WORLD

Post-modernism rapidly became an international movement, and one of the leading European practitioners was the Austrian architect Hans Hollein (*b.*'34). Throughout the 20th century, architects were just as involved in the interiors of buildings as their exteriors, and Hollein's most famous design was for the interior of the Austrian Travel Bureau (Vienna, '76–78). With travel as his theme, Hollein's imagination ran riot – his design included a gold-roofed Indian pavilion, flying birds suspended from the ceiling, gilded palm trees, a broken classical column, and the railings of an ocean liner (complete with lifebuoy)!

A vast, 43-metre-long, golden sculpture crowns Philippe Starck's surreal design for the Asahi Beer Company's headquarters (Super Dry Hall, Tokyo, '89). The building is clad in black granite, and the sculpture was made by shipbuilders using submarine-construction techniques.

The curved form of this stunning post-modern skyscraper echoes the bend of the riverbank it sits on (333 Wacker Drive, Kohn Petersen Fox Associates, Chicago, '81–83).

FUTURE VISION

Throughout the 20th century, people tried to predict how technology would shape future lifestyles. During the '80s and '90s, these futuristic visions were dominated by the oppressive landscape of the cult film *Blade Runner* (Ridley Scott, '82).

The columns and arches of Charles Moore's Piazza d'Italia pay tribute to the architectural styles of ancient Greece and Rome (New Orleans, '75–79). Moore's post-modern twist is to decorate his structure with vibrant colour, stainless steel and even neon lights!

The futuristic city created for Blade Runner *is nightmarishly chaotic and overcrowded.*

INSIDE-OUT BUILDINGS

Another unusual architectural style was developed during the '70s. Called 'high-tech' because of its focus on engineering and construction, it was more technologically orientated than post-modernism. The results were just as playful, though, with buildings literally being turned inside out!

The Pompidou Centre is an arts complex which houses a library, galleries, museum and research centre. According to its architects, its colourful, inside-out design made it look like 'a giant Meccano set' (Rogers & Piano, Paris, '71–77).

HIGH-TECH ARTS CENTRE

The world's most famous high-tech building was created in the heart of Paris in the early '70s, by the British architect Richard Rogers (*b*.'33) and the Italian Renzo Piano (*b*.'27). Called the Pompidou Centre, it is remarkable because its structural skeleton and all its services are on the outside. Huge, colour-coded pipes carry the services, with air conditioning and heating in blue pipes, water in green, and electrical systems in yellow. The lift blocks are red, while the external escalators are protected from the weather by transparent tubes. The external skeleton means that the interior is completely free of structural supports, and the huge, open-plan floors are subdivided only by movable partitions.

In his steel and polished concrete Lloyds building, Rogers again freed internal spaces by positioning lifts and staircases on the outside (London, '78–86).

18

HIGH-TECH GOES HIGH-RISE

The 179-metre-high Hong Kong and Shanghai Bank is another innovative high-tech building. It was designed by British architect Norman Foster (b.'35) and hangs from external, tubular-steel masts which rise the full height of the building. The masts are connected by suspension trusses which look and work rather like coat-hangers – the building's main floors are suspended from them.

MAKING STEEL STRUCTURES SAFE

The heat of a fire makes steel lose its strength, so to protect them against fire, the steel parts of a building are either encased in concrete (1), wrapped in heat-resistant panels (2), or sprayed with a fireproof substance (3). Another method was used in the Pompidou Centre – to absorb heat energy and keep them cool, the tube-shaped, steel supporting beams were filled with water (4).

1   2   3   4

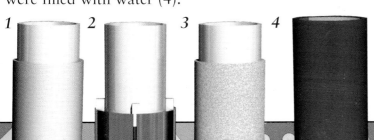

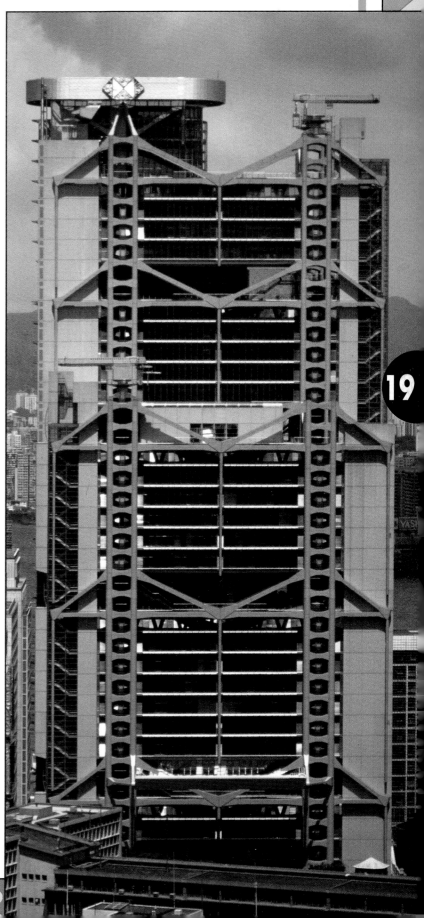

19

NFORMATION TECHNOLOGY

When the first electronic computers were built in the final years of World War II ('39–45), they were huge, room-sized machines. By the early '70s, technological advances had led to a new age of miniaturized electronic components – and the development of the microprocessor.

Computers have revolutionized life in the office and at home.

MINIATURE CONTROL CENTRE

A microprocessor is a microchip (or group of microchips) that controls all of a computer's operations. It is the central processing unit (CPU) or 'brain' of a computer, and the first to be marketed was the Intel 4004, launched in '71 in the United States by the Intel Corporation.

A microchip is a tiny sliver of silicon containing the thousands of components that make an electronic circuit.

20

Founded in '76, Apple's first PC was the Apple 1. The Mackintosh, or Mac, was introduced in '84. Its styling was created by the German group frogdesign (f.'69).

CHIPS WITH EVERYTHING

Microprocessor chips meant smaller, cheaper computers, and they paved the way for the introduction of the PC, or personal computer, in the mid-'70s and early '80s. Soon microchips were controlling everything from traffic lights to washing machines.

LASER TECHNOLOGY

The laser was another invention that had an enormous impact on daily life. A number of scientists worked on its development, but the first working laser was built in '60 by the American engineer Theodore Maiman (*b*.'27). Computer printers now use laser technology, as do bar-code scanners (first used in '74) and compact discs (developed in the early '80s). In communications, laser beams now carry telephone, computer and TV signals along optical-fibre cables. The technology was developed in the '60s and early '70s, and the first optical-fibre trunk cable for telecommunications was installed in '76. A single, 10-millimetre-thick cable is made up of 100 fibres, and can carry as much information as 20,000 of the old, copper telephone wires.

Lasers are used in many ways, from cutting, drilling and measuring to satellite tracking, eye surgery and holography.

OPTICAL-FIBRE TECHNOLOGY

Optical fibres exploit the property of light waves to refract, or change direction, when they pass from one medium to another. A single optical fibre is a flexible, hair-like strand of highly refractive glass or plastic covered by a less refractive cladding. The covering acts as a mirror, so that light is continually bounced back into the fibre's core. A laser device is used to transform electrical digital pulses into light pulses at one end of the fibre. They are reversed at the other end by a device called a photo-detector.

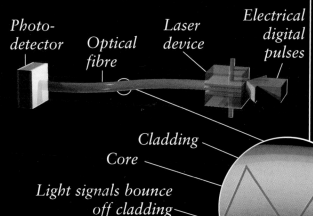

Photo-detector   *Optical fibre*   *Laser device*   *Electrical digital pulses*

Cladding
Core

Light signals bounce off cladding

CHIPS AND LCDs

The microprocessor chip revolutionized the manufacture of electronic devices, and chips came to be used in a huge range of products in addition to computers. Calculators, typewriters, video-cameras and cassette recorders, televisions, telephones, washing machines, microwave ovens and even cars were all transformed by them.

In the '80s, the Swiss company Swatch made colourful watches, powered by vibrations from a quartz crystal, into must-have fashion accessories.

VIDEO WAR GAMES
The first home video-cassette recorders were marketed in the early '70s. In '76, new systems were launched by two Japanese competitors. A battle for market leadership followed, which was won when JVC's VHS (video home system) ousted Sony's Betamax.

In video-cameras, sound and images are recorded on magnetic videotape.

SMALL IS BEAUTIFUL
The miniaturization of electronic components meant that the housing of a product need no longer be affected by its inner workings. Industrial designers were free to go to town on product styling, and a new era dawned in which gadgets became as much fashion statements as functional objects.

JAPANESE TREND SETTERS
The leader in this field was the Japanese company Sony, which was responsible for one of the first electronic fashion accessories, the personal stereo. The idea for the Walkman is said to have been dreamt up by Sony chairman and founder Akio Morita while playing tennis.

Launched in '79, and styled by the Sony Design Centre, the Sony Walkman was the first personal cassette player. Its styling continues to evolve today, in line with changing fashions.

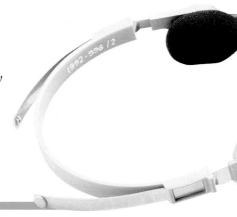

22

This compact portable electronic typewriter was styled by the Italian architect-designer Mario Bellini (b.'35) for the Italian manufacturers, Olivetti (ETP55, '87).

The German designer Dieter Rams (b.'32) styled this pocket calculator, with a liquid crystal display, for the Braun company in the late '70s.

MYSTERIOUS CRYSTALS

Another technological breakthrough of the period was also transforming electronic gadgets. Scientists discovered liquid crystals back in the 1850s, but the first practical ones were not developed until the early 1970s. Liquid crystal displays (LCDs) are wafer thin and need very little power. Soon they were being used in watches and pocket calculators, and from the '90s, in laptop computers.

Liquid crystal display

LIQUID CRYSTAL TECHNOLOGY

A black-and-white LCD is made up of groups of electrode segments. Inside each segment, liquid crystals are sandwiched between pairs of polarizing filters (like the ones in Polaroid sunglasses) and transparent electrodes. The filters are at right angles to each other, and when there is no electric charge the crystals twist light so it passes through both filters and reflects off the mirror – no image is displayed. Applying an electric charge changes the crystals so they stop the light from passing through the bottom filter – a black image is displayed. Numbers and characters are formed by applying charges to groups of segments.

Light

Light

Polarizing sheet

Transparent electrode

Liquid crystals

Transparent electrode

Polarizing sheet

Mirror

Charge applied – no light reflected

No charge – light reflected

ALTERNATIVE TRANSPORT

In 1973, OPEC (the Organization of Petroleum Exporting Countries) raised oil prices by more than 200 per cent and began restricting oil production. The fuel shortages that resulted caused an economic crisis in industrial nations all over the world.

In Brazil, the oil crisis revived research into making car fuel out of alcohol distilled from fermented sugarcane juice.

24

GREEN MOVEMENTS

The oil crisis fed the growing concern about the Earth's natural resources, prompting increased support both for environmental movements and for research into alternative technologies. Greenpeace had been formed in '71 by Canadian opponents of nuclear testing, and in '79, the world's first Green political party was founded in West Germany.

Maglev trains are propelled by electro-magnets. The technology was developed in Britain, Japan and Germany, and the first maglevs began running during the '70s.

MLU 002

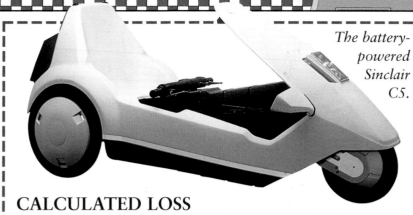

The battery-powered Sinclair C5.

CALCULATED LOSS

British inventor Clive Sinclair (*b.*'40) made the first truly pocket-sized calculator in '72, and later manufactured personal computers. His battery-powered Sinclair C5 ('85) was less successful – production stopped within months.

In '79 an American team achieved the first pedal-powered flight across the English Channel in this plane, Gossamer Albatross. Their next plane, Solar Challenger, combined pedalling with solar power.

The world's first transcontinental race for solar-powered cars was held in '87, in Australia.

GREEN POWER

Fossil fuels such as oil are not only non-renewable, they cause pollution, and in the '70s and '80s research was carried out into all sorts of renewable, 'clean' power sources – including solar, wind, wave and tidal energy.

GREEN TRANSPORT

Alternative transport was developed, too, with engineers working on everything from electric (battery-powered) cars to solar cars and planes.

In rail transport, one of the chief wastes of energy is caused by the rubbing effect of the friction between train wheels and track. Maglev is short for 'magnetic levitation' and maglev trains reduce friction by floating above the track. They were one of the most exciting developments since the invention of the steam train.

THE SCIENCE OF LEVITATION

The maglev system exploits the fact that the like (positive or negative) poles of a magnet repel, while opposite poles attract. Maglevs use powerful levitation and driving electro-magnets, with one set of each sort in the track and the other in the train. In most maglevs, levitation comes from using like magnetic poles to repel each other, forcing train and track apart. Drive comes from alternating positive and negative poles. Positive poles in the track ahead pull (attract) the train forward. As it passes over the track's negative poles, the maglev is then pushed (repelled) onwards.

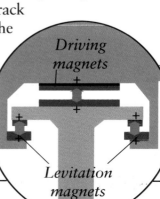

Driving magnets

Levitation magnets

HIGH-TECH PEOPLE MOVERS

Although the basic shape of most airliners has barely changed since the 1950s, a revolution has taken place in their construction. One '70s and '80s innovation was the use of high-tech materials such as carbon-fibre-reinforced plastics. Another was the introduction of computerized control systems.

The A320 was first flown on 22 February 1987.

Strong, light, high-tech materials save fuel by helping to reduce weight. They were widely used in the A320, for everything from wings and tailfin to brakes and engine mountings.

THE FLYING COMPUTER

Built by Airbus Industries and first flown in '87, the A320 was the first passenger plane to have computerized, fly-by-wire technology. In the past, pilots controlled a plane's movements manually, through a large, central joystick. In a fly-by-wire plane, a small side-stick is connected to a flight computer, which 'reads' the side-stick's movements and controls the plane electronically. Nearly everything on the A320 was computerized – computers told the crew where they were, what condition they were in, and even where they were likely to end up!

Airbus Industries is an international group of companies, each of which made part of the A320 in its own country. This special plane, the Guppy, *transported the parts for final assembly in Toulouse, France.*

ROBOTS – FROM TOY TO WORKMATE

Although mechanical automata were being made as long ago as ancient Greek times, the word robot wasn't coined until 1920 – the Czech playwright Karel Capek created it from the Czech *robota*, meaning 'forced labour'. The first robot able to use a tool (for painting) was put to work in Norway in '66. Since then, computer-controlled robots have been developed which do everything from brain surgery to playing the piano and shearing a sheep!

Since the '60s, industrial robots have been designed to carry out tasks such as welding and assembling electronic parts.

HIGH-SPEED LAND TRANSPORT

Maglevs may one day be the world's fastest trains – in '97, a Japanese maglev reached 401 km/h on a test track – but back in the '70s and '80s, the fastest way for land passengers to travel was in electric trains. These trains take electricity from overhead cables and use it to power traction motors which drive their wheels. They have doubled the speed record of 201 km/h set by the British steam locomotive *Mallard* in '38. In '88, the German ICE electric train reached 406 km/h, while in '90, the French TGV (*Train à Grande Vitesse*) managed an astonishing 515 km/h!

The French high-speed electric train, the TGV, was brought into service in '81. Its usual operating speed was about 210 km/h.

The British high-speed electric train, the 125, entered service in '76. Its exterior was styled by the British industrial designer Kenneth Grange (b.'29).

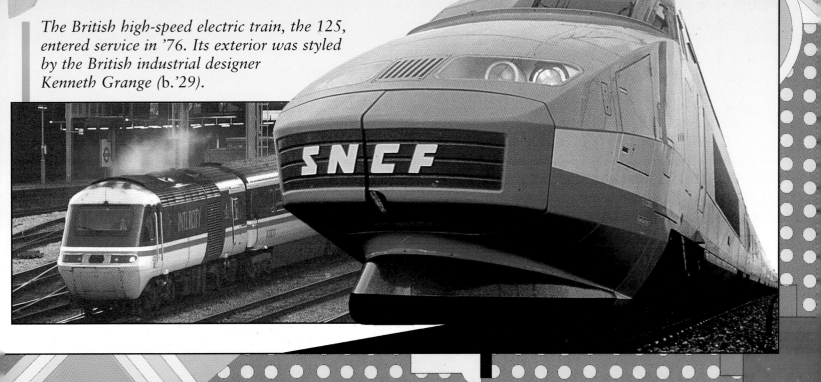

SPACE TRAVEL

Space exploration made giant leaps forward at this time, boosted by technological developments. The United States and the USSR continued to launch unmanned spacecraft in the '70s – they both sent probes to Venus and Mars, while the Americans also sent probes to Mercury and to Jupiter and the other gas giants.

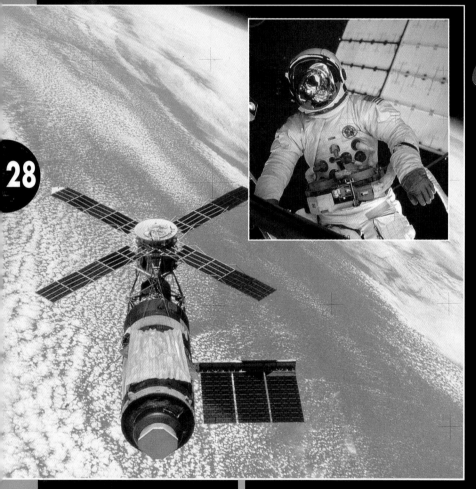

Two Voyager probes were launched in '79. Both visited Jupiter and Saturn in '79–81, then set course for Uranus ('86), Neptune ('89), and the edge of the solar system.

REMOTE-CONTROL ACTIVITY

Once in space, the probes were powered mainly by solar panels, although gas jets were used to make course corrections. Commands were sent via radio, from Earth to on-board computers.

SPACE WORKERS

Both the USSR and the United States also built space robots. Two robot landers were sent down to the surface of Mars from the American Viking probes in '76, while two Soviet Venera landers scooped up soil samples from Venus in '81. The Soviets and the Americans were exploring the possibility of sending human explorers into space, too. In '71 the USSR sent the first of a number of manned Salyut space stations into Earth orbit, followed in '86 by Mir. The United States launched their only crewed space station, Skylab, in '73.

Launched in '73, the American space station Skylab completed three missions before an attempt to shift its orbit made it fall back to Earth in '78. It was destroyed by the atmosphere.

THE PRICE OF SUCCESS

The United States lagged behind the USSR in space station technology, and the main reason for this was money. NASA's budget was being swallowed up in developing the space shuttle – by the time the first shuttle, Columbia, was launched in '81, the programme had cost nearly US$10 billion! The space shuttle was revolutionary, though – it took off like a rocket, cruised like a spacecraft, and landed like a glider. And although its vast external fuel tank burnt ten times as much fuel as a jumbo jet, it was the world's first reuseable spacecraft.

Two Viking landers touched down on Mars in '76. They photographed the planet's surface, reported on its weather, and tested soil samples for signs of life.

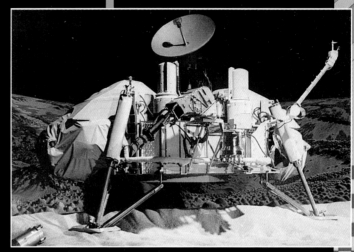

THREE-STAGE JOURNEY FOR A REVOLUTIONARY SPACE MACHINE

The space shuttle has three main parts – the orbiter, solid fuel rocket boosters (SRBs) and an external (liquid fuel) tank (ET). The orbiter carries the crew and the payload. At lift-off (1), the orbiter and SRBs are attached to the ET, with the SRBs providing most of the thrust. The SRBs are released soon after lift-off and parachute down to the ocean to be collected and reused. The ET is jettisoned as the orbiter reaches orbit, and is destroyed by heat as it falls through Earth's atmosphere. In space, the orbiter is used for scientific experiments and for launching satellites (2) and other equipment. As it re-enters the atmosphere, the orbiter is protected by around 23,000 heat-resistant ceramic-coated tiles. It glides back down to Earth to land on a runway (3).

1

2

3

29

GLOSSARY

CARBON FIBRE A thread of pure carbon, which is very strong and stiff. Carbon fibres are made by heating textile fibres such as acrylics in the absence of air. They are used in fibre-reinforced plastics to make strong, lightweight materials.

FORMICA The trademark of a heat-resistant plastic laminate.

FRICTION In science, the force that slows moving objects down. It is caused by two surfaces rubbing against each other.

GRAPHIC DESIGNER Someone who designs type and images for printed materials.

HIGH-TECH In architecture and design, a style that celebrates technology, which emerged in the 1970s. 'High-tech' can also mean the use of advanced materials or equipment.

INDUSTRIAL DESIGNER Someone who designs products that will be made by machines.

LAMINATE A material made by bonding together thin sheets of one or more other materials.

LASER A device first built by Theodore Maiman in 1960, which produces a very powerful, narrow beam of light.

MICROPROCESSOR The central processing unit (CPU) or brain of a computer, which controls all the computer's calculations. A microprocessor may be one microchip or a group of chips.

MODERNISM An international movement in architecture and design that emerged in the early 20th century. Rejecting historical styles and unnecessary decoration, modernists believed that the appearance of an object or building should be determined by its use.

OPTICAL FIBRE A very thin, transparent, flexible fibre of glass or plastic.

POST-MODERNISM A worldwide movement in architecture and design that emerged in the 1960s and '70s in reaction to modernism. Colour, decoration and an eclectic mix of historical styles were embraced.

PROTOTYPE A test model for a new product.

RECESSION A time of economic difficulty which is usually less severe than a depression.

TITANIUM A strong, lightweight metal which is resistant to corrosion (wearing away by air, water or chemicals).

30

DESIGN HIGHLIGHTS

- *Shiro Kuramata's irregular furniture* — 1
- *Vivienne Westwood opens her first shop* — 1
- *Richard Sapper's Tizio table lamp* — 1
- *Issey Miyake has first fashion show in Paris* — 1
- *Des-in studio: Tire sofa* — 1
- *Jamie Reid art directs Sex Pistols* — 1
- *Kenneth Grange styles high-speed 125 train* — 1
- *Rogers & Piano: Pompidou Centre* — 1
- *Philip Johnson begins AT&T skyscraper* — 1
- *Charles Moore's Piazza d'Italia completed* — 1
- *Gae Aulenti: Table With Wheels* — 1
- *Memphis design group founded* — 1
- *Tadao Ando: Kidosaki House, Tokyo* — 1
- *E. Sottsass: Bay lamp*
- *Swatch watch* — 1
- *James Dyson: G Force bagless vacuum cleaner* — 1
- *Michael Graves: Kettle with bird* — 1
- *Richard Rogers' Lloyds Building opens* — 1
- *Tom Dixon: S chair* — 1
- *Starck: Royalton Hotel, New York* — 1
- *Design Museum opens in London* — 1

TIMELINE

	WORLD EVENTS	TECHNOLOGY	FAMOUS PEOPLE	ART & MEDIA
0	•US troops sent into Cambodia		•The Beatles split •Deaths of Janis Joplin & Jimi Hendrix	•Germaine Greer: The Female Eunuch
1	•Uganda: Amin in power •Greenpeace founded	•First microprocessor & space station (USSR's Salyut 1)	•Muhammad Ali loses world heavyweight title to Frazier	•David Bowie: Starman •Kubrick: Clockwork Orange
2	•Direct rule in Ulster •US troops leave Vietnam	•First video game & pocket calculator on sale	•Mark Spitz wins seven golds at Munich Olympics	•Francis Ford Coppola: The Godfather
3	•Middle East: Yom Kippur War; oil crisis	•US Skylab space station launched	•President Salvador Allende of Chile assassinated	•Thomas Pynchon: Gravity's Rainbow
4	•Turkey invades Cyprus, occupying one third	•Bar-code scanners first used in supermarkets	•US President Nixon resigns over Watergate scandal	•Fellini: Amarcord •ABBA: Waterloo
5	•Cambodia overrun by Pol Pot's Khmer Rouge	•First small home computer, the Altair, sold	•Bill Gates & Paul Allen found Microsoft	•Steven Spielberg: Jaws •Queen: Bohemian Rhapsody
6	•S. Africa: Soweto uprising	•First fibre-optic trunk cable for telecommunications	•Steven Jobs & Steven Wozniak found Apple Co.	•Christo: Running Fence environmental sculpture
7	•UN bans arms sales to S. Africa	•First human-powered flight, in Gossamer Condor	•Steve Biko dies in S. African police custody	•Sex Pistols's God Save the Queen banned by BBC
8	•Egypt & Israel sign Camp David peace treaty		•Louise Brown, first test-tube baby born	•John Travolta stars in Saturday Night Fever
9	•Iran: Khomeini in power •USSR invade Afghanistan	•Sony Walkman first marketed	•Thatcher becomes Britain's first woman prime minister	•Woody Allen: Manhattan
0	•Start of Iran-Iraq War •Poland: Solidarity set up	•First portable computer, the Sharp PC 1211	•John Lennon shot	•Anthony Burgess: Earthly Powers
1	•Egypt: President Sadat assassinated	•First space shuttle, Columbia, launched in US	•Prince Charles and Lady Diana marry	•Rushdie: Midnight's Children •The Face launched
2	•Falklands War between Britain & Argentina	•First artificial heart is transplanted	•Death of Princess Grace of Monaco	•Ridley Scott: Blade Runner •Spielberg: E.T.
3	•US & Caribbean troops invade Grenada	•CDs first go on sale •AIDS virus isolated	•Lech Walesa awarded Nobel Peace Prize	•Merce Cunningham: Quartets, dance pieces
4	•New Zealand declared a nuclear-free zone	•Apple Mac launched, styled by frogdesign	•Bob Geldorf sets up Bandaid pop charity	•Madonna: Like a Virgin •Philip Glass: Akhnaten
5	•USSR: Gorbachev becomes leader	•Battery-powered Sinclair C5 •Ozone layer hole confirmed	•Death of Orson Welles	•Lucien Freud: Self-Portrait •Arvo Pärt: Stabat Mater
6	•Chernobyl nuclear disaster in USSR	•Space shuttle Challenger explodes	•Cory Aquino wins Philippines elections	•Jeff Koons: Rabbit
7	•Black Monday stock market crash	•First flight of fly-by-wire A320 plane	•Terry Waite taken hostage in Beirut	•Toni Morrison: Beloved
8	•End of Iran-Iraq War •Lockerbie air disaster	•Stephen Hawking: A Brief History of Time	•Benazir Bhutto prime minister of Pakistan	•Iris Murdoch: The Book and the Brotherhood
9	•China: Tiananmen Square massacre	•Nintendo launch Game Boy video game	•Khomeini issues fatwa against Salman Rushdie	•Helen Chadwick: Enfleshings

31

INDEX